WELCOME . . .

. . . to the world of Paula Morgan, whose poetry will have you nodding your head in recognition, wiping a few tears away, and smiling through them. And just when you think she's sentimental, you'll come across a poem that makes her seem hard as nails. Which she is, when she isn't soft as butter . . . just like you . . . and me . . . and just about everybody else. Paula Morgan lives through everything that happens to all of us. The difference is that in her unforgettable verse she is able to make us aware of the universality of those experiences, to share all those splendid and not-so-splendid moments that are common to us all . . .

ATTENTION: SCHOOLS AND CORPORATIONS
PINNACLE Books are available at quantity discounts
with bulk purchases for educational, business or special
promotional use. For further details, please write to:
SPECIAL SALES MANAGER, Pinnacle Books, Inc., 271
Madison Ave., Suite 904, New York, NY 10016.

WRITE FOR OUR FREE CATALOG

If there is a Pinnacle Book you want—and you cannot
find it locally—it is available from us simply by sending
the title and price plus 75¢ to cover mailing and
handling costs to:

Pinnacle Books, Inc.
Reader Service Department
1430 Broadway
New York, NY 10018

Please allow 6 weeks for delivery.

_____Check here if you want to receive our catalog
regularly.

Say Yes!

by Paula Morgan

PINNACLE BOOKS   LOS ANGELES

Portions of *Say Yes!* have appeared in
The Roses Have Never Wilted
© 1975 by Harris Publishing Company,
Beverly Hills, California;
Pieces of Myself © 1976 by
Harris Publishing Company,
Beverly Hills, California

The Tennessee Williams quotation on page x
is from *Summer and Smoke* and used here with
permission of the author.

This is a work of fiction. All the characters and events portrayed in this book are fictional, and any resemblance to real people or incidents is purely coincidental.

SAY YES!

Copyright © 1977 by Paula Morgan

All rights reserved, including the right to reproduce this book or portions thereof in any form.

A Pinnacle Books edition, published by special arrangement with Quadrangle/The New York Times Book Company, Inc.

First printing, March 1981

ISBN: 0-523-41408-0

Cover photograph by Brian Leng

Printed in the United States of America

PINNACLE BOOKS, INC.
1430 Broadway
New York, New York 10018

*For my Father
and
Mother*

For my dear family and friends who
have weathered all the storms and have stayed
to applaud even when yours was the only
sound—I love you all.

And for the booksellers all over America
who were kind enough to put me on counters
and in windows; without
you nothing would have happened. Here we go again.

Paula Morgan

Contents

Me	3
Together	5
Lessons	7
Surprise	9
Marriage 1970s	11
My Son	12
Lisa Beth	13
An Ode to My Phone	14
Waiting	16
America's Hero	17
The Other Woman	18
Shrinks	20
Life	21
Rhea	26
My Mother	28
Making Rounds	29
Looking at Pictures	31
Saturday Father	32
An Ode to Bobby Short	34
The Great Middle Age Jewish Conspiracy	35

10 Minutes Terrific 37

You're On, Kid 40

Special Girl 41

Sleepless 43

$30 Haircut 45

Madmen 47

Fear No More 49

Stop 51

George C. Scott 54

That Girl 56

Power Thy Name Is Money 58

For Shepsie! 60

His Hand 62

Leonard 64

My Brother 65

No More Birthdays 66

25 Years 68

Elaine 70

Say Yes! Please! 71

Merry Go Round 72

The Pattern 73

What's Better? 75

Two Alones 77

The Man in the Dark Green Suit 79

Leah 80

There Are Hours 81

Amy	83
Gayle, Gayle	85
Hello! New Friend	87
Goodbye Take Care	88
Things	90
Dick	94
Salek	95
Cologne?	97
Where Do I Come From?	99
Rain	100
Sheila	102
Suicide	103
Nothing	105
Camp	106
Group Therapy	108
Theatre	110
Who Am I?	112
Maybe Tomorrow	115
Depressed	117
No Nos	118
Thursday	119
Mother's Day	122
Father's Day	124
Women's Lib—Yes or No	126
Television	128
Yellow Roses	131

Ask for all, but
expect nothing—only
the coming true of
your most impossible
dreams.

—Tennessee Williams

Say Yes!

Me

I never read the Koran
　　　smoked hash
　　　known EST
　　　　　or
　　　biofeedback
Or spent one minute
　　　contemplating
What I came in
　　　knowing
I never needed to
　　　learn
And what I could
　　　have used
No one ever taught
　　　　　Me
I'm not even street smart
I am a believer
I never think I'm being taken
Tho' I know I am
There are days that my anxiety pounds
In my fist and sits on my chest so
Hard I can hardly breathe
There are days I am quite beautiful
And on a bad compulsive day
　　　Ugly
　　　Ugly

Every once in a while a special light
Shines on me for a moment
Just long enough to make me totally
Mad forever
         I am like you
         full of confidence and fear
         both at the same time
I want to survive—better and longer
And to do it with style
I have a love affair with life
         with my family
         and my friends
         and my kids—most of all
I am your mother
I am your lover
I am your child
I am a woman
         I am like you
         and we are
             the same!

Together

They came together
They were beautiful
Full of hope
Full of the stories of America, America
Gold in the streets

They came from
       pogroms—no Jews allowed
       ghettos' poverty—2000 years
       of living in one place—fear

They came from culture too—and music and a kind of
Arrogance
       they were the chosen
       they would endure
       they would survive
       they would succeed

It was hard. There was depression, war—a big war
       ovens, crematoriums, ghettos—only Jews allowed
       they survived
       they dreamed
       they fought
       they succeeded—Jews were now allowed

There was a country—a flag—there was an army,

and a new generation began
     they were still together
     they were old
     they were alive
     they were still together

How does that happen? This is 1977.

Lessons

What is there about us
We are not a moment like our
Mothers
        they married
        bore children and
        stayed with our fathers
        despite—
          forever
But We
        We love
        We marry
        We bear children
        and We search for
        new fathers for our children
        new ways to live
          over and over again
Our mothers
        tried so hard for us
        they said
        learn
        be free
        be strong
        have purpose

We did all that
        But We
            didn't learn patience
                    or
                    forgiveness
        We
            didn't learn
            how to make it work
        We are not our mothers
So here We are
        brilliant
        sophisticated
We know everything
        We stand at our windows
        night turning to day
        a lifetime gone
            and how do We stand?
            We stand alone!

Surprise

The ballroom was huge. It was the most beautiful gold
    room
I'd ever seen
A princess in a palace
It was a Monday
We were in love
It was my birthday
It was New York.

The band began to play and we danced and whirled and
It was a glorious surprise, he had asked the hotel to fix the
Room and hired the band. Just for us, just we two.
He was Gilbert Roland, and I was Mata Hari
Lalique glasses and French champagne
        And streamers, all colors
        And the 2 of us.

There was a box from Tiffany's all wrapped in grey velvet
A hansom cab down 5th Avenue . . . I was Gloria
Swanson and Garbo and God—he was—well . . . he was

And time came and days passed and the streamers were
Hung for someone else and the hansom cab was hired by
    another
Couple who took another ride down 5th Avenue
And I cried

And I cried
And I bought two hats
And I went to Ardens
And I looked
And I looked
He was gone forever.

And then a friend came, and I saw Ethel Merman sing,
    "Roses Turn" in *Gypsy*
And I kept the box
And I lost the man
And I never saw him again—except in my head
And I never forgot the ballroom.

I keep looking for it.

Marriage 1970s

Now, what is marriage anyway?
I always thought it was Dorothy Maguire and Robert
Young in *Claudia*.
And when I found out it wasn't, well, a sadness
Came into my tower.
The part of the wife was always played by Ruth Hussey.
(Now who wants to be Ruth Hussey, except Ruth Hus-
sey)
The other woman was Carole Lombard—of course,
That's better.
So marriage was Carole Lombard at Bonwits
Being pursued by a misunderstood husband
And his little girl loved "them" and hated her mean mama
Who was big in charities, and smoked and was never home.
He couldn't get a divorce—and Carole was too good to
Be kept

That's what marriage was, either Ruth Hussey or Dorothy
Maguire—but, never, Carole Lombard. The other alterna-
tives were
      1. Married and bored
      2. Being alone
      3. Being kept
      4. Raising children alone and being kept
      5. Or remarrying, raising children alone and
         helping to keep your husband
It's 1977
And only the names have been changed. The alternatives
are
The same, only with more bravado and we're all alone any-
way
      Maybe I should get a job at Bonwits

My Son

My son used to ask me how he was born and I have always
Told the same story—
I asked for a friend.
I asked God for a special child—a child with blue eyes
And a wide smile and my very, very own
      And God listened
      And he was born
      And I was never lonely again
Now he is older and he knows how he was born
But my reasons are even stronger now
He is all I could want
He is filled with energy, and curiosity, and eyes
That fill with tears when hard truths come
      He is an enormous joy
      He is a reason for believing in life and birth and
        truth
Please, my son. Don't be different. Don't let the world
  change
What you are . . . I couldn't stand it.
You are still not just a son. But a friend I asked for . . .
      Maybe there is a God!

Lisa Beth

Lisa Beth—
    My survivor
How are you
How are you
      You came from pain
      You came from love
      You came when a marriage was over
      You are terrific
      You were so small
      I could hardly breathe every time
      I looked at you
      So glad you came
      You have given me so much strength
      I look at you and I am the world
      You were so needed
      A mother needs a daughter
      I love your face
      I Love You
      You have made it all worthwhile

      You are a survivor
      You are mine
      You Are Me!

An Ode to My Phone

My telephone
       is really everything!
It is life's exercise
So much happens on it!
       I cannot live without it
       It is my truest friend.
Where else can you hear everything
You'll ever need to know about—anything—
       In an instant!
I cannot even think of any form of life without it
What do people do—stranded—
       No telephone!
Darwin would've had a telephone theory
Who will ever forget "smiling Don Ameche"
       And pale Loretta Young
       And their story
       My God
       How gorgeous.
You may call me anything you like
       But call me!
Leave me alone—forever—
But . . . give me a good, clean telephone
And . . . I am again, revived, reborn, alive.

Can I give it a medal
Can I kiss it? No . . . but
I can tell you—anything—everything—
With my 'phone.
Just think of . . . Martha Mitchell, Louella, and Hedda,
Joan, and Clare Booth Luce,
Without a 'phone—
That we cannot do without
forever and ever
Amen!

Waiting

—So glad you came
    your pictures
    are terrific
—I mean this is a great shot

—Your reading
    was really great
    we hope we'll
    be able to use you
—You look marvelous
—Now, don't call us,
    we'll call you

I waited
And I waited
They Never

                Called

America's Hero

He hated graft, McCarthy, and Fascism
He loved Scotch, cigarettes, and brains
America, the great middle west,
And being a celebrity
His voice said "This is London"
And the world stopped and listened

He said hello to me—and I stopped
It was a long hello—he never said goodbye
It was "goodnight and good luck"

He was Ed Murrow
And I was never the
same again.

The Other Woman

The other woman
      sleeps till 12:00
      takes 3 hours to dress
      doesn't jump out of the shower
      to get a bottle,
      or change a pair of pants
      because
      she is childless.

The other woman
      is . . . kind, sweet, loving, and,
      never has a headache,
      because
      She doesn't have a head.
      She is always calm, serene, smiling
      she can tell your husband, as she mixes a martini
      that he is marvelous
      because
      she's never lived with him, yet
      She smells of "joy"
      she is seductive
      she wears new lingerie
      she even has a clean purse—without cookie crumbs
      because
      she has only . . . herself.

I have more than myself—I am very busy!
If I ever had 3 minutes
        I could smell of "joy"
        I could wear white pants, and be seductive.
If he wants her,
good luck to them both
        she is a bore
        she is a clean, new toy
        (how lucky can you be)
I know—I'm a real *woman*
        part mother
        part toy
        and a lot of person
        if that's not enough
Goodbye.

Shrinks

In my group everyone who is anyone has one

Now, first you have your own
Then your husband (if you have one), has one
Your kids, then, have theirs—individually, of course
Then, there are group plans (like an airline ticket sale)

Now, can you imagine the dough these people are making?
Is it really helpful, does it work, anyway, it takes
a lot of time, it's great conversation and it is deductible
—if you can prove to the I.R.S. that you really need it
Now, that can be damaging, maybe later, depending
On what schools your kids plan to attend, if any

Shrinks really are similar—thoughtful, elegant, cool,
detached, and r-i-c-h—and they l-i-s-t-e-n.
I have a cousin who was, and is, a holy terror, and he's
the high priest of Bedford Drive, it's because he has
John L. Lewis Eyebrows, and smokes a pipe—l-i-s-t-e-n-s.

All this money to learn to enjoy a hot dog?

Life

Laughing
> Running
> Jumping
> Crying
>> Not thinking
>> Just doing
> Small-sized persons
>> Living every moment
> Hanging from bars
> Standing on heads
> Bodies stretching
> Shouting
>> Childhood—
>>> Marvelous
>> Adolescence—
>>> Difficult
>>> Minds sharp
>>> Silly
>>> Angry

Not men yet, but not children anymore
> Important time
> Then high school—
Medium-sized people
> Thoughtful
> Carrying books
> Grumbling

Screaming,
Tests, points, papers
Dirty tennis shoes
Beautiful skirts
Long hair
Funny jeans
Thinking, doing, preparing
College
Driving
Drinking
Smoking
Thinking
Term papers
Lectures
The Future
Credits
Units
Tuition
The wrong girl
The right boy
Theosophy
Marches
Protests
Degrees
Speeches

The Future
Graduate school
A practice
Money
Or lack of it
Worry
Today is tuff
Study
Work
Think a lot
Dream a little
Work, work, work
Quiet
The Future
When will it come
Marriage—
The rat race
Baby coming
Mortgages
Work, save
Banks, loans
Taxes
Fear
Body not stretching, not like before
A quiet shouting, inside

Is this what it's
All about?
Children growing
Age coming—age is here damn it
Dreams
 Some succeed
 Some not
Questions—
 Maybe to drop out
 Is this what I did all of
 That for
  Is this what I
  Wanted
   Questions
   Discontent
   Boredom
Remembering—
 That playground
 and
 A childhood
 to
 Prepare me
For what?
 To get old
 and
 Tired

But
Did I do
What I
Thought I would
and
Did I become
What I wanted
and
With whom
Or was I so told how to live that
I never had a chance
To just do
and
Just be
and
Now it's too late
The voyage here is almost over and
I can remember pieces of
What was once
My memory has begun to fail now
And I guess
So have I
But then
So have we all
Is that all there Is?

Rhea

Rhea is an original
I mean with whom you can share
  lox and cream cheese
  or go to Loehmann's
Rhea is abrasive
  Intolerant
  Opinionated
  Hostile
  And quite horrible
  Who would go to all the trouble of
  going to the hall of records
  to find out exactly how old I am—you know the
   kind
  We all have one!
We met when all the laughter had left me and
She stayed to keep me laughing so hard
I forgot my pain
  With this lady
   You can steal
   Forge a prescription
   Maybe even discuss the Talmud
I guess she's part of my life, damn it—the
part I'd like to forget—and
  somehow keep remembering

Don't we all need someone
to make sure our feet are
never off the ground!
Everyone does—
It's part of being human
Having
an insulting
difficult
simply marvelous
ego-stripping
Friend

My Mother

She is a paisley shawl
        a black jet tiara
        and the Eyes of all the Jewish Martyrs
She never played Pan, belonged to the P.T.A.
        drove a car pool, or baked cookies
She did take us early to opera and lectures and concerts
        Culture . . . culture . . . culture . . . !
She is the original believer
        In women's rights
        Abortion
        Birth control
        Divorce
She believes in Me.
She is the atypical Jewish Mother
        She is a child of Europe
        She could never be called an immigrant
        Though she was
She is a Lady
She is My Mother. She cares in Her own way
        I care in Mine

Making Rounds

I look back on all that
Wondering *how* I did it
I know *why*
      I wanted that gold ring
      I wanted the star on that door
      I wanted the applause
And for that
      I preened
      I dieted
      I studied
      I walked—oh! I walked
I spent the madness of my youth
Asking strangers to tell me I was special
Asking a world to take me in that wanted to keep me out
I wanted all of that rejection
I needed all of that acceptance
      And I was not alone
      A whole city seemed caught up
        And was
Oh! I got a piece of that ring
I got a bit of star
      Was it enough
      Was it worth all of that
        Pain?

I don't know worth
I do know love
        Yes! for me
        It was what I had to do
        It was all I knew then
        I don't know much more now
I know it is a time to remember
That adventure
The real time of my growing
                up!

Looking at Pictures

Looking at pictures is a mistake
Today I look awful
     In the pictures I look great
Today every line shows
     In the pictures it's always beauty, color and smiling
Today is bleak
     and empty
Yesterday looks so terrific
Better than it was in kodachrome
Better than it was in ektachrome
       Better than it can be in life
       Now, what will tomorrow be
       If yesterday was beautiful
       And today is cold
       What is tomorrow
       Can it be worse than today?
Emile Coue said "Every day and every way
we get better and better"
     To be a Christian Scientist and believe that.

Saturday Father

We once loved
We fought
Oh, how we fought.
We once loved
And then it died
There was no more fight, or hate, or anxiety
There was emptiness.

Now he comes . . . and he loves them . . . as best he
  can,
And he buys toys and games, and hamburgers, and they
  wait
To see him and be with him.
        and He tried
        and I hoped
        and It died
We share nothing, neither time, nor friends, nor
Experience, nor even laughter
His feelings for me are guarded, and empty, and angry
        A quiet anger.

His going and coming used to be terrible. Not any more
It's almost a relief. How does that happen
        That once we loved
        Then we died?
It's the years of the lack of care, the lack of sharing.
I wonder what will become of him . . . he seems such a
Wanderer . . . he answers nothing, he asks nothing, he
  seems
To want nothing.

But I am a woman
Who lived with a man
And loved a man
And bore him children
And believed in dreams
I thought we would fight forever.
But now I have given up, there is really nothing left.
Even my hope for what could have been is gone—not
For anything I can name, but everything I can't
Name, or can't feel.

I am a woman
And he is a man
But we did love
And tho' It died
And It cannot be
I did feel once that I cared
Perhaps those moments are what love is

It would be a miracle to start again, to forget all
The empty yesterdays, but
He would have to look at me, and see me, and know me
And he won't. Maybe he can't. It's too bad.

I am a woman
Who loved a man
Indeed
I did. I did.

An Ode to Bobby Short

"Let there be you"
        Dear man
"Let there be me."
        You were my
introduction to
        Rogers and Hart
        Mabel Mercer
        and
        What was left of the Cotton Club.
When you took me home one night
A man in blue
Said Hey! do you live here
If you don't you don't belong
And I remember I said you belonged to me
And the man in blue walked away
        You continue to give me joy
And I continue to believe that you
Belong to me
        And so does everyone who has ever heard you!

The Great Middle-Age
Jewish Conspiracy

You're supposed to be married no matter what
You're supposed to have children who aren't just
    children
    But super achievers
    Inventors, doctors, lawyers, rich . . . rich
You're supposed to be pretty, wear a size 10, and
    cope.

Now it doesn't really matter if you have colitis, an ulcer,
And you really don't like your husband.
We are super women, we are great, we cope.
Do we . . . do we ever . . .

We support every medium, fat doctor, astrologer, psychia-
    trist,
Plastic surgeon from here to Long Beach.
We are not found in bars, or hotel rooms but at macrame
Sessions—understand your whole potential—
At lunch for Reiss Davis, U.J.A., bonds for Israel, excep-
    tional
children, spastic children, gifted children, O.R.T., Hadas-
    sah,
Etc. Etc. and So Forth.
Most of my ladies live in their cars. It's called
Mommy's limousine service, to lessons, lessons, lessons
But what happened to the graduates of Bennington and
    Columbia
and Bryn Mawr? Are we fulfilled?

And the marriages great—and romantic—and rewarding—
>   Or is time going
>   And dreams passing
>   And age coming
>   And husbands waning
>   Is it really worth it—is there a way out?
What if I'm not home, or he misses his lesson
When did I last walk down La Cienega romantically
With someone, anyone
When did I not worry about rashes and flat feet and
>   Braces and school
Why not run away, run away . . . and dream of
>   Just dream
How would they be without me—I don't know.

>   I am responsible
>   I am Jewish
>   I have super achievers
>   I wear a size 10
>   I have a waning husband
>   And I cope
>   Oh! I cope
>   Isn't that terrific

10 Minutes
Terrific

I saw him
Standing alone
     White pants
     Yellow windbreaker
     Black hair
     A pipe
I had never seen
     him before
maybe
     a hundred times
I was alone
We looked
My mind said
Forget it
     He'll have a wife
       or he had a wife
He sees his kids on Sunday
     If I look back
     because he's cute
It will all start
Again
The love
The pain
And the anger

Is it better for
       10 Minutes Terrific
        To have love
        Pain
        Anger
To start again
I don't know
I'm too scared
I got up
I started walking **to**
       the door
The room was very
       noisy
But, for an instant
       our eyes met
I stopped
I looked at him

My, my—he looked at me
We said nothing
We both know
     it was pow
     For 10 Minutes

Terrific

It Seemed Not Worth It—
     Am I Wrong

You're On, Kid

For Myself

It only takes a moment
> For all the yesterdays and their pains
> To go away with those words,
>> "you're on, kid"
> all of a moment you can feel your face
> light up and that candle in your soul
> burning
> you just lost 30 pounds
>> you dropped 10 years
>> suddenly grew 5 inches
> And it didn't even take a sentence—just three
>> words
>> that heat is flowing inside
>> when the audience says
>>> I love you
> To feel that way by yourself, without an audience
> that would be—marvelous
> but that's not possible—is it?
> the lights
> the camera
> the great smell of pancake

Heaven
> who said it's for nothing
>> it's for
>>>> everything!

Special Girl

When I was 5
> he walked into my measles bedroom . . . in his
> black tuxedo . . . young . . . my face filled
> with calamine . . . and kissed me

When I was 8
> my mother was in Europe
> He took me to Bullock's Wilshire, bought me a
> blue coat trimmed in velvet, and took me to
> Perino's to lunch
> and told me I was his special girl

When I was 14
> He took me to N.Y., told me there's a great
> world out there, took me to Saks, bought me
> a suit from London and told me I was pretty
> and I believed it

When I was 17
> He said, o.k., you want to be an actress
> so, go be
> but you have a contract with me
> and I was on my way

He came to all the openings
He was there at all the closings
He told me I was swell, no matter what.
When everything around me said,
> "No"!

He said,
> "Yes"!

He said they are fools—they don't know.
When I married someone he wasn't sure of, and had my
　　son
He said, I'll help you, and he did
When I had my baby girl, and the marriage was finished
He said, you're O.K. by me,
When I said, marriage and I are not compatible
He yelled, but he said, O.K.
I want to make him know somehow
　　　　That no matter what happens next
　　　　I walk very tall
　　　　I can really handle everything
I believe I can because he believes in me
　　　　and it sure helps, doesn't it.

Sleepless

Who are all the people in the picture-perfect houses
Who can turn out the lights and fall asleep
They must have beautiful bedrooms . . . beautiful lives . . .
      and beautiful husbands
I have none of these
But in my house live beautiful people—in faded chairs
      that need redoing
But very bright lives
So why can't I sleep
It's because I'm lonely
Lonely for someone to buy pretty sheets for
Or a new nightie
Or even share the late show
Well! . . . it's not going to happen tonight
So, I'd better stop thinking
And look again at my beautiful people
And tell myself maybe tomorrow—
And try and sleep

Someone asked me if I am ever lonely
I always say, No! . . . No!
      I'm fine
      I am a liar
I don't dare let myself remember I am lonely
Or I'll crack
And I don't like that

I only remember I am fine
I am always fine no matter what
Who are all those pretty people
Who fall asleep as soon as the lights go out and never stare
          at the dark
Are they a special form of human?
They must be
Everyone I know is like me
Oh! there goes the phone
Someone else who can't sleep
Hello! . . . Hello!
Wrong number
I'm getting tired now
It's almost morning

Thank God, and Seconal

Good night.

$30 Haircut

You know
      that feeling
something
      marvelous
      will happen
You stand in
the mirror
      all the colors
        in place
      looking at yourself
A minute ago
      I looked rather
      awful
And at this moment
      all the age
        has gone away
Can't a good girdle
      and a $30 Haircut
        do wonders
Tonight
      I'm going to hear Sinatra
      Here I am a middle-aged
      bobby-soxer getting ready
        to swoon
Is it to relive my youth
      Was it all that wonderful?

And since
        I'm the only one around my answer
        must be Yes
No one will know I'm there
But I will, and for an instant
        I've forgotten all the
        pain
        All that
        time
I'm a bobby-soxer all over again
        Not wiser
        Not older
        but young
                and
        free
                and . . .
That impossible time
        The clock has stopped
        and I am new
        all new
        With only the regrets in my head
        not my face
Yeah, a $30 Haircut is a miracle.

Madmen

I used to think
madmen were
concentrated armies
   or
movements
   or
causes—
I used to be a child
I'm not anymore
    now
Madmen everywhere
stopping us from feeling
  bombs everywhere
  lockers and planes
There's no place to run anymore
What does a mother
tell her children
Who read it—and see it?
on the tube
Not the Viet war dead or
The Korean plane count or
How many were gassed at Treblinka
But our own streets
what happened to that world
where we stayed
innocent forever?

My fear of death
for those I love
is all too close now
Anxiety sits in my chest
       waiting
We wake up every day so shocked
we no longer
assume that man
has passed through
the dark ages! We know he has not
Is there no end
We must just try and live
and not think
Maybe our turn
     won't come!
Maybe it will go away
like a bad dream
     "Somewhere
       Over the Rainbow."

Fear No More

She held his
        hand so tightly
        joyful, excited
        frightened, but
        secure
She was in the
        ocean
        for the first
        time, and he
        was showing
        her how
He told her
the ocean was
her friend
She believed him
She screamed
        with laughter
She screamed
        with joy
He turned to me
        waiting and
        watching on
        the shore
and said
        O.K. Ma

And as I watched them
        together
            The waves
            lightly brushing
            them
        I could feel
        my beach robe
        wet
            not with
            the ocean
            but with a mother's
            happy tears
They are
        happy, he is
        helping her
        learn the
            world
            I have
            taught him
            well—he
            has learned
            all the lessons
He will help her
He will hold her hand
            I was very
                happy.

Stop

They say it is
　　　better than Auschwitz.
　　　is it?
They say we show the
world our strength
　　　do we?
They say we fight
we are not afraid
we are Jews
We will survive
　　　will we?
Cannot a voice
　　　a voice of reason
a mother's pain
a bloody face
a tank blown in bits.
Does it matter
　　　whose?
Does it matter
whose son fell first?
They are too young
　　　to die
It is all wrong
Does no one hear
　　　the anguish
　　　　of the mothers

Who bear the sons—
who must bury
            them too—
Is all reason
            gone
Is oil, my son,
more important than
you are?

You are more worthy,
you are part of me,
I die when you die
            stop
            stop
The price is too much
I cannot endure
the suffering
            —and if we
            win
The lines of
boxes will never
            stop

Someone listen
            we are burying
            our sons—

Life is no
        longer worth
        anything—
            is it?
If life is
        worth nothing,
        and death is
        without honor—
        then what is
        it all about?
            Someone listen.
And stop this madness.

    we beg you

George C. Scott

There is a conspiracy in this country
That men are unromantic
Rather dull
Agressive
Money wanters
Moneymakers
Money spenders.
Now, let us discuss George C. Scott.
I was not a fan of General Patton
—Or of any military man
But, George C. Scott in *Petulia*
With his broken nose, spindly legs, neck like a truck
  driver,
And, in his shorts
Well
He is a man!
He made me forget poems, prose, and my intellect.
I mean he was, and is, gorgeous
He is midwestern, an actor, much married
But *gevalt*—I'd change it all
All my middle-class ideologies about men
With that beast—Scott—
I notice Coleen Dewhurst married him twice!
Now marriage is not my favorite
But you can't lose too much with him—I mean really—
I notice Julie Christie has never been the same

I'd even start saluting the flag
For
    George C.
      And that's a lot
        For even Scott!

That Girl

It sometimes flashes through
I see that girl
        walking up that sidewalk
in New York
        everything moving
            so much
                excitement
                energy and
                    confidence.
I see that girl
        And when I do—I sometimes wonder
what happened to her
Did she really have
All of that energy
        or was it New York's
            special amphetamine?
                And did all that hope
go away with the years?
        Did it get watered down?
        Did she get acceptable
and grown up?
I look at her in my mind's eye
and I think wow!

You thought you had it all
Your way didn't you kid
It was going to be
Saturday night forever
          and you could get in and out
of everything
couldn't you?
I think I'll leave you in my head
where I find you
          Even if I met you now I'd
               look at you and say
How lucky you are
Such passion for life!
I wonder if you knew kid
that the sidewalk
you walked was not
the yellow brick road.
No! it was only a sidewalk
But when next we meet
          I'm not going to tell you.
I want you to remember it
          as only you can
          Because you're very special
You're my youth.

Power Thy Name Is Money

I came face up today
to the power structure
      in a building like a mausoleum
      with a desk full of Tiffany ashtrays
and Steuben Glass, immaculate and orderly
There sat a man who can control peoples' lives
He was not a man
      not anymore!
A man has soul
      This man was
a super-oiled, plastic-based, well-made
      machine
His eyes were not blue, no, the color of steel
      As I looked at him I realized
he really had nothing
Only what his money could buy
And I wondered how much love had been bought today
      Kafka was right, he was the
      man who had become the machine
        and I don't know how to talk to
        a machine
        never again will I try

How dreadful to have all that power unless
it gives joy and love. And if I ever thought
I'd like some
      No! No! God,
        Listen
No power, please—
I met a man without a soul today and I will
never forget it!
      Soul is one luxury
      I can afford.

For Shepsie!

Our dialogue consists of
1. "What's there to eat?"
2. "I need to go to the library"
3. "Make an appointment with the dentist"
4. "Do you know about hypnosis?"
5. "Don't bother me"
6. "Finals this week"
   "I said close the door"
That beautiful baby boy
  is now an adolescent
You know what that means
It means—involved with self
All the social amenities are gone
   It's all growing
   and glands moving
   But he's very interesting
    when I do see him
   He's brimming with
    Anger
    Ideas
    Energy
    Curiosity
Books say if you live through this
   Well! I got through all the rest
   But this one
    is a test

It's not terrible yet
But it's on the way
      Please adolescence
         hurry—and go away
         I'm not young enough
to go through all that
      Is that what age appropriate means
      Well!
         Mine isn't!
There are moments
when I see the man
you are going to be
      It fills me with so much joy, and wonder
How lucky to be
         Your Mother.

His Hand

For Zayde

I remember his hand
    all freckled
    old, plump
        and in mine
He was a Hasid
And on Yom Kippur
as he prayed in that old shul as if Yom Kippur were his
    his white beard and black coat
    that look of him
    his concentration on his God
    the wisdom of the sages
    I would wave at him from the window but he
        would
    eye me sharply
He had many children and grandchildren
But I was his favorite
As I got older and started
questioning his God
    he even tolerated that!
When it was time for him to go, and the angel Gabriel
had called, it was very late, he was ready

He gave me his hand
His hand was in mine until that last
          moment
I will never forget that feeling
as I write now I can see it—his hand
          all
          freckled
          plump
          and
          warm
            and in mine.

Leonard

Your life has order
            mine has not.
Your life is yours alone
            and mine is not.
You seem hard and invulnerable
while everything about me is open,
            like a huge trunk for anyone to see.
You are close-mouthed,
and yourself.
How are we friends? It was so long ago
at the St. Regis.
Our first date lasted twelve hours—my—
Yet, you have never loved me.
that has always bothered me.
            I cannot find you out
            and I have stopped trying.
You have always protected me,
been both cynical and kind.
It is a badge of honor to have you as my friend.
How I smile when I think of our days in the saloons
            and how many times you have bailed me out
            when I had nowhere to turn.
I hope I have brought you joy.
I know—I am a headache,
            and of everyone I have ever known
            I would trust you with my life.

My Brother—I'm Sorry Jerry

When I was little, I thought he was everything.
When I got bigger he was every intellectual proletarian
    hero
I thought he was a world saver
An idealist
A thinker
He spoke with big words, and had red books
His books were red, very red
And so were his thoughts
And he married the wrong
girl, and I was
sad.
The first real disappointment
Do we ever get over that, ever? No matter how many
joys may follow. Never. Never.
It's a locked, unspoken pain. It's a teacher to start guard-
    ing
your heart.

I hate it.
I love him still.
My brother.

No More
Birthdays

What is a birthday?
For our children
it seems they have passed
another stage of life and time
and it is so festive
Their life is a huge balloon
       Happy Birthday!
I want not to be remembered
a day older than maybe yesterday
It's an indignity
to give a woman a party
at 40
       Why advertise
       that the trip is nearly over?
We should start a movement
       Girl children have
       parties 'til 21
       Boy babies
       maybe 30
       That's enough
I have forgotten my birthday
       And I'm sure my mother
       will never tell
       If she did
       she'd lie

If I get to a hundred
          maybe then
But until then
          the candles are
          for the children
I hate that commercial
          "I'm not getting older,
          I'm getting better"
Better for what?
Dietrich says
          "A woman that will tell her age
          will tell anything" and I wouldn't
          want to argue with her
Am I afraid of age?
          Isn't everybody?
                    Amen

25 Years

The anniversary is supposed to celebrate
25 years of togetherness
      Now what does that mean?
      I mean in light years
        It means about four wars
        The kids get grown and go away
        The chairs get redone many times
        You buy a lot of season tickets
        By that time
which means all communication has stopped
      (we talk between acts now)
You start thinking about lifting your face
And when you finally get that trip to Europe
to visit the graves of the greats,
your husband says "it's cold—let's
get out of here"
And it is really cold—everywhere!

68

25 years
And the trip you worked so hard for
is such a bore
Now Hallmark may bomb me
But I think we should take a personal vote
          and abolish anniversary, forget time
after all
          25 years is totally enough,
               don't you think
We served our time
Now
let's serve ourselves
a slice of truth
Let's have a day that is honest
really honest
That's the best anniversary
          And anyway you are still my friend.

Elaine

It's about that time of the year
It seems a moment ago
I knew nothing about death till you died
I don't know anything about it now
One minute we were laughing
The next minute you weren't
I see you all the time
In my mind's eye
Smiling, and laughing, smoking Pall Malls in your big red
   car
And shouting "hurry . . . hurry"
I miss you
Everyone does
You left too soon
There was more of life to do
The time we had was precious and fun
I think somehow—you know—I think of you and always
   will
You haven't really gone
You wouldn't do that
Without telling me first.

Say Yes! Please!

I look back—
        because when the swells happen it's
        impossible to stop and register it all
        When it all stops then I can reflect
I forget sometimes how many no's I've heard—
        how many tears I have shed—when the no's
        came always, at the worst time or for the
        best things
Sometimes I forget and just remember the good
It's easier
I never thought pain was necessary to build
        my character
        only my character lines
I always thought acceptance was the best
        and it is—I want all little children to have
        instant acceptance, so that twenty years later
        they won't have to spend their lives on black
        leather couches talking to a special form of human
        called a shrink—who really can't fix it anyway—
Not without our help!
No one can
Only ourselves
        Say Yes!
          Please!

The Merry-Go-Round

Don't you love the merry-go-round?
Don't you love to catch the brass ring?
Even when you know it's only brass
I love to spin, go up and down
Listening to the music
'Round and 'round, never stopping
My merry-go-round stopped . . .
And I got off
The brass ring turned black so fast
I forgot that it was ever gold

Someone said it was time to get off
Someone said find something real
It's better for you
Is it? I loved the ride, I could have gone
On forever and never would have known the
Difference . . . would I?
       I did love the ride . . . I hope I won't be sorry

Why did I ever listen to that someone
I did love that ride.

The Pattern

For Gussie

There is something
wrong
Something wrong with
        the pattern
            I mean life and death
We pass through
        all that beginning
when we are young
        and beautiful
Strong enough
        to fight for
            money and identity
And just when
we can finally finally stop
        All of our fighting
        age comes
        Then sickness
        and the game
        is all over
Everything we are
Everything we've learned
Gone
        into a box
            Finished

And it took
such a short time
There must be a
        way to do it
that it lasts longer
That the longer is
        better
            That it doesn't
            end with a
            few tears and
            a damned box
The pattern is all wrong
There must be
something we don't
know
        Somewhere
        maybe
Shangri-La
In the Valley of
the Blue Moon
        James Hilton
        You knew
        Didn't you.

What's Better?

If sex was better than
  almond rocca
If sex was better than
  lox and cream cheese,
now that it's all so free and accessible,
Then why do millions keep running madly to
  "Weight Watchers"
  "Be Thin"
  Diet Doctors
  Diet Pills
  Diet Shots
Well, doesn't that tell us something? It does me
I must tell you
  Masters and Johnson never asked me anything
  Kinsey was confused
  and Freud was misguided.
Every mother knows
  Cocoa calms the nerves
  Rice takes care of the stomach
  And chicken soup can cure anything
Then our conclusion must be that food is
  terrific
  That sex is questionable
  And if you have a choice—

If it were my last day
        I'd spend it eating
            Wouldn't you?
Now, let me decide what
        and where
        so I can
        plan
        ahead
        when that
        day comes
            Listen,
            without
            it being
            my last
            day,
                I could
                start
                right
                now
Couldn't You?

Two Alones

I am so jealous of
        Those couples
        in their jeans
        and boots
        walking together
        so close
Walking down tiny streets
        smiling
Looking into windows
        small interesting windows
        and
        talking to each other
        really talking
That always stuns me
They seem as if they care
that whole look of them
Nothing in their pasts
to guard them
against being free with one another
        How did we go away so fast?
The old jeans almost fit
but the texture of us
is not the same
We hold hands
and look into windows
not really speaking!

Not really looking, into each other
            but just those windows
Anything outside is better than
            to stop
            and
            ache
                for what
                is no longer
                part of
                us!
Why do we live this way
Is it easier?
holding hands and
not really holding hands
is holding no one
So
            here we are
Two alones
            walking together
            Time passing
            Years lost
I hate the picture
            He must too

A Man in a
Dark Green Suit

Why do we choose
what we choose
He was tall, and his eyes were blue, and there was some-
    thing in his walk
A laugh, human
A special way of looking at things
A special way of looking at me.

He was safe.
        And we did love
        We did, we did.
        Will we again?
        Does anything ever end!

Time has not changed the color of his eyes—but
the way he looks at me is not the same.
He does not laugh any more!
The years have not been kind to him—
        Does he love someone else
        Does he love himself
Will he ever be the same again?
Questions . . . that cannot be answered. Maybe
it's better not to ask. But, I wonder. I wonder.
He was awfully cute in the dark green suit.

Leah

Her face was
      patrician
Her walk
      tall and straight
      She was well boned
        and well born
I always thought she
      belonged to live
      at a different
      time
Her name was Leah
She was not like other grandmothers
      She wore chiffon
      in the kitchen and she spoke of things
      alien to her generation
I don't know if she believed
all that religious tradition
      She did adore me and I thought
      she was a queen
      She did not live to see my children
      She would have liked what she would have seen
      In her world that had seen so much tragedy
      she was a heroine
I wonder if much of what she was didn't rub
off on me
      No! I just stopped wondering
       I know it did!

There Are Hours

Sometimes
when baby is asleep
My son gone
House quiet
2 hard hours
      —I drink the wine
      —I eat the food
      —Watch the news alone
The day was fine, so much to do
But the nights
      —one is fine
      —some are not
      —some nights don't matter
      —people call
      —no one matters
      —no one I want
      —no one I need
      —no one who matters
Will it ever matter?
      —another wine
      —is this why people drink?
      —I could answer
I don't

I could be high on
    a fellow
I say no
    I don't know why
This is my time
If anything mattered
    I'd answer
Oh! finally
    a sound
    The two hours
    must have passed
      Baby's up—
      The phone rang
    it's my son
The empty space
    is over for now
    Do you have any
    empty space
    Doesn't everybody

Amy

I see you in your blue
coverall
age 2
   blonde curls
and little ivory face
   different
At 11
you wore funny jeans
and you were nature's child
   eager
   shy, falling
   over yourself like a puppy
I have always watched you
   Your aloneness
   And that temper
   And your poetry
   too timid to tell it
   or show it
But I have heard much
   of what you write
   And I know who you are
   I only hope you do
Yesterday, still at 15
   blonde and
   with that ivory face
   but almost a woman

A thrill rushed onto
        me—Amy
        I can't see that woman
        that you are finding in you
I want only to see the
        child in
        the coverall
        and to
        beg you
        to stay
            no matter what the pain
        Different from the others
            because
            you are

Gayle, Gayle

You are the earth mother
Tho' you must believe in fantasy
      if you believe in me
Behind your eyes I see
      mostly clouds
The smile does not give you away
      But the eyes,
      Do I read right?
I always thought
happiness is
exactly what you have
      if not you
then who of us could claim that?
      I would call on you for anything
But to whom do you call?
And when you need
who bathes your need in love
      The children
      The husband
      Really,
      Who?
Questions I should not ask
I have
      You never answer
because
      "no answer is also an answer"

And you are not the only one like you
You are one of many friends
who bury their yearnings,
      put them away
      for later. When does later come?
      No,
        please,
           don't
           don't answer
I want not to know
      and so do you.

Hello! New Friend

Hello! new friend
    You had a special sound
    that made me feel
    my madness was
    welcome
    And even tho' we'd never met—you
    were not a mystery
I who fright easily
and cover it with noise
    suddenly,
        when we did meet
    I knew I had nothing
        to cover
    You seem kind
    and sensitive to my
    fear of losing
        what has taken a lifetime
        for me to grasp
    And I have found
    something special
        not just
        for today
    but for all the new tomorrows
    We'll need to investigate
Hello! New Friend.

Goodbye
Take Care

We have lived with
life's best dividend,
          our children
But just long enough
to get them ready to go away
To leave us
To be persons
          away from us
          away from our
          special umbrellas
We prepare them
But who prepares us?
To see them only when
they come home to visit.
I think I hate that
I hate the whole idea of
cherished independence
I would like them
near me
          until they find
those partners that might put them
under their own special umbrellas
to keep them safe

But I am selfish
          old fashioned
          and a fool
And this minute the thought that
they will soon fly away is too
much for me
Oh! my God
          I just saw them
          walking out the
          door.
                Oy! Gevalt
Goodbye Take Care

Things

There are all kinds of ways
to lose oneself
      there's TM
      (I never know what to
      meditate about, and if
      I ever think about what
      I am trying to avoid
      I won't make it 'til Tuesday)
And
Biofeedback (that's got wires)
EST (how smart they are)
Yoga—supposed to
      be good for sex, all those positions—
      but everyone looks so pure
      (its tough to
      do yoga in
      the A.M.
      and
      come home to
      a dirty kitchen)
Gestalt (very German)
Freud (anti-women)
Modern combinations (madness)
Primal (hard on the throat)
Group (dull-dull)
Conjoin (boring)

Berne's games (when you stop playing
          whadaya do then)
Self realization (too simple)
3 H's (Happy Healthy Holy)
protein only
          (powder naturally
          to get rid of feelings
          of anger and hostility)
Sensuality (you gotta have it)
Bi-sensuality (even better)
Abstinence (impossible)
Fasting (even worse)
Body cleansing (OK)
Gravitation exercises (you gotta understand it)
Group sex (gotta have a group)
          my God, a hundred
          ways to lose
          yourself and start again
With what, please?
          With yourself,
          poorer
          thinner
          and cleaner
          and confused
No more junk foods
or junk thoughts

A higher level
        Yes!
But my question
remains
If you are on a
        higher level
        and your environment
        stays the same
What does your
        higher level do?
        It makes you feel
        awful that's what
And if you were
trying to cope
        with the help
        of pills—
        and now they've
        all been cast aside
        (bad bad pills)
        in favor of looking
        at life
        alert
        awake, no longer
        drugged,
It's an awful trauma—
I have decided to
regress

To go back to
junk everything
and face the world
        slightly drugged with
        a feeling of euphoria
Not thinking about
anything
        Hoping tomorrow
        will be better
I'm going back to smoking
with the threat of cancer
and allied diseases
Reality can kill
        you faster than anything

Addenda
        My seven-year-old just
        threw out all of my pills
As a token of her love
        And my son has
        put a ban on smoking
        in the house
        Couldn't you just
die?

Dick

I saw you
> young
> blond
> tall—handsome and

Aryan
> I was frightened—
> and charmed too!
> As the years passed
> since that seamy elevator
>> on 46th Street years ago

Our backgrounds so different
Your parents different from mine
> Catholic

We became friends
You showed me a new way of
> laughing at life

And in my deep heart
I often wonder if things had been different
> What might have been

Your talent has always
> amazed me, and so have you

You have sometimes changed
> my whole day—with a
>> special cymbidium just
>> for me—you are no longer
>> Aryan—

We are the same

Salek

Old
Shy really
Sitting
       talking to a banker
As I watched him
It seemed
       seconds had passed
       when he'd sat talking
         not shy
       to statesmen
       men of literature
       men of power
He was younger
He had confidence
       but
He still had all his papers
in a plain rubber band
There were flashes today of the frightened
young immigrant, who could not speak the language
       all earnest
       trying to please
I could hardly keep my eyes from tearing

Watching
      just looking at him
All of what he owned
      and owed
All of what he had
      fought so hard
to keep—
      All he had come with—
      and all he would leave
      All of it—all of it
        in a plain rubber band

Cologne?

Our survival of this time—my god!
15 years—is more than a puzzlement
It is a combination
        of everything
It is our eternal war with life
        Parents ill
        Children
            who
            need
            us
            both
With disappointment and success we took
hands for reasons each of us cannot
remember
We have come through life's war
        Is that love?
        or endurance
What is marriage anyway?
        I don't know
Is it a time to merely partner one's problems?
Even apart we have been together

We should have ended
years ago
          Everyone said so
          they still do
          maybe we'll surprise
          ourselves and last
          wouldn't that be a
          miracle
But then
          this whole trip is one big
          mirage—and we're still
          traveling, aren't we?
            It could be that I like
            your cologne

Where Do I Come From?

For Edith

I come from 5,000 years of ethics
I come from pogroms and ovens
      where my murderers
      charted and graphed
      my death scenes
I am a survivor
I come knowing you don't want me
I come knowing I will make you need me
      I am a Jew
If you let me I can show you who I am
If you kill me something of me will survive
Without me
You have emptiness
      Then there is no ethic
      I did not choose
      to be what I am
But no matter
I have survived it all
      And you
      have you survived your guilt?
Or is there nothing in you that cries
      for what you have done
You must take a lesson from me—
      I never forget
It is part of what I am
      I am a survivor
      I am a Jew

Rain

The best days are
        the ones when
        it rains outside
And inside you
        it's all warm
The rain, God's special surprise,
        lets me think
        of things
            Seeing New York for
            the first time
                A rainy cold Sunday
            And the stores
                all asleep
                gray, the streets quiet
        Steam coming off the roofs
                out of small restaurants
                couples sat, drinking
                talking
                looking at the city
            And the first time I
            said goodbye to Daddy
                Dearborn Station
                Chicago
            The rain pounding on the windows
            of that train
And my silly plaid coat wet with my tears

The him that was once
lost to the rains—that night in Paris
the walk we had
after we decided to love one another
That first time, raining on the beach
That forever rain the night
my son was born to
Such a long vigil and
The morning rain
my daughter was born in
It rained for days
I used to tell my children
rain was the time God was crying
I know now that when He looks at the
children of the world
They must be
tears of
happiness
Why else
would everything good
happen when it rains?
Rain is the whole world renewing itself
starting again
trying just once more
That's the story of
my life
Trying just once more

Sheila

Imagine
Looking like East Hampton
   and coming from Brooklyn
Maybe she should have been Maya Plisetskaya
She seems all alone
The world too big for her to swallow
She is my friend
I want to help. I try
Maybe life is easier when we're less dreamlike
   and accept things as they are
Maybe it helps to know husbands don't change
That children grow up and go away
I always wanted to be willowy—no, it's better to be
   a truck
I roll easier
Sheila, Sheila, look around you
We never know our blessings 'til they've gone away
You might find another willow and intertwine
But you won't if you don't know how beautiful
   you bloom

Suicide

I love the rain
I love the theatre and its forever magic
I love being warm, and needed, and loved
I love my children, and the look of them asleep, all secure
I love the sounds of the mornings, and my father's walk
    coming up the steps with his hard thump, and the *sound of*
    the rattling of packages
I love feeling high on my own energy
Excited about a dress, or a party, or a place
It's good to have friends who really, really care
    whether they approve or not, they care
I like brains, and beauty, and guts.
I don't know about the love of a man . . . I like it . . .
    But I've
    been so disappointed, I don't know how I feel
I like anticipation, and humor, and performance, and old
    movies, and new dreams
I bless my mother for giving me the energy to keep fighting
    in myself what could depress rather than make me go.

I hate suicide
it's so gutless
I hate giving up or giving in—or selling out
I loathe compromise, and ignorance, and inflexibility
I don't know if it's a Jewish ethic or my own
    But a way of living that tells me one's own way must be
    the way.
There is none other for me.
It's better to be alive than dead
It's better to suffer and struggle and be in pain than give
    up
For 5000 years Jews were told to give up and somehow they
    didn't, or couldn't, or wouldn't, and they endured
And there is pain, and struggle,
But there is life
And life we can go with
and do
and be
or try
Why not live just for the sake of living
                              Good Morning

Nothing

I wanted you to make tonight something I would
long remember and tuck in the back of my eyes
when I thought of you
You seemed exactly what I had waited so long for
You were going to kiss away my fear
and I was going to be
      young and pretty
      all over again—you were all new
We tried
      and something happened
      The way you looked at
        me
      No, you never looked at me
        You never saw who I was
I was just one more you had found and conquered
        But even that didn't happen
        Was it because I was as a child, or that you
        could not free yourself to hold me?
        It doesn't matter—nothing does—
So here I am, foolish,
        Lonely once again

Camp

I have grown a man
        A boy no longer
        No more burps
        Nor fear of the
            dark—
        Our voices need
            not cross
        tho' I miss your
            voice
This is the beginning
    of goodbye
I have tried
I have given all
I know—and most
I hope you'll never
        need
            You are yourself
            your road is
            your own
            clear
            and ahead
As I stand watching
        you go
The time has come
        too soon

The time has gone
        too fast
        Is 12 so big?
        Is 12 a man?
Yes! my son you
are on your
        way—alone
        Secure
        Straight
I have grown myself a man
        Goodbye—
        I could die

Group Therapy

Group anything has got to be awful
I went to a super group therapy group. I mean it
was so super I had to wait three months to get in.
The doctor, who looked like a huge myna bird, was the
    head of everything. He had been trained everywhere.
And each person was hand picked by sex,
style or neurosis.
The room was so perfect—the set from
Lady in the Dark—only better.
After telling our names—first only—the group asked
What we were thinking
        I said
            Spin the bottle
            And an English muffin!
aha. aha he said—deep anxiety. Obviously post-
natal depression brought on by a need for dependency on
your mother. (Are you ready for that?)
The other people had swell ones like murder—
    homosexuality
or parental approval, distrust or paranoia.

It's true my marriage was in a lot of trouble
My son was too smart and most unusual
My daughter is a Jewish princess
—but these people;
They were really sick
They didn't see the sky or the clouds or life
They didn't even laugh
What a waste of time.
Unless I were reborn a Nordic saint they couldn't help
    my madness
No . . . I think I'll keep my madness.

No one else wants it.
Maybe we should have played spin the bottle.

Theatre

Moss Hart said
        "It was the fantasy
        of the unhappy child"
Then what has the happy child?
Any better
or more rewarding
being on it?
        In it
        or going to it?
The happy child—
Hurray for him
He has none of those yearnings,
That damn stage
        makes you feel
        and forget
        who you are, and you lose
        yourself, you become someone else
I always thought
to stand on a proscenium
and spout words
of Williams or Chekhov
was a miracle

And those people—
        My kind—the best kind
Forever children
        really
It's like
        being with a "band of angels"
        who somehow are alike
The play is the thing
It's that secure
insecure feeling
        to go at 8:00—somewhere—and find that you belong.
Your other life
        is away from you

For a moment in your life
        you too can forget
        who you are!
And we are both blessed

Who Am I?

I always thought I was
        big and dark
    until reality's mirror
    showed me I was small
       and not dark at all
    Without the cosmetic bottle
    I would be but flush red!
I have always made my face
a porcelain shell
    when really I am one big freckle
forever hiding my spots under
       big hats
       and creams
       and darkened rooms
Those who knew me
       when,
       and see me now
       say to others
       in whispers
        "she" looked—
not how "she" was or is.

       I am now what I
am expected to be
       porcelainized
       and dark

With only small glimpses
of age to disturb my
pictured sameness
My red mouth
  everpresent
So friends who do not look for age
remember me as I was
And do not notice
  my soul too frightened
  for my mouth
  to change

why am I what I think
I should be
And not what life's mirror
tells me that I am?
Is it because I yearn to please
  those whose years
  cannot be hidden?
And those whose time sits not
too kindly with them?
Or is it for myself?
The never ending riddle
  of what is or what was or if it ever was really
I cannot remember.

I must stay the clock
As long as it will
give me space to
move its hands
Now or before
          back then
          or
          tomorrow
I will sleep quickly
remembering I must be
          who I am
          tomorrow
      Someone could see
      me—and not
      know me—
          and I would
          be alone—
      without even
      today for
      company.

Maybe Tomorrow

I wanted to run away today
    Just not think about
    The market!
    or
    The kids!
    or
    Anything
I wanted to go on this
cold gray day
    and sit on the beach
    with someone
    And I called
    all the someones I knew
    and
    everyone was out
    too busy
They didn't really want to
    They too
    "had too much to do"
Why do we have so much to do
That we never do what we really want
    Is that grown up?
    And responsible?

What fool said
        "It's better to be responsible"
Maybe in my silliness
        I thought
        I could be responsible when I wanted
And then when I didn't
        run away
Now I'm getting like the others
Am I not also responsible
        for my own joy?
            I only wanted to run away for today
            But now the clock says
            it's too late
Time to pick up
Time to be a mommy again
The time for me is over
        for now
Maybe tomorrow
        "No!"
Tomorrow I've got too much to do
        There I go
        again
        Plans that I made for me
        Gone—away
Have I lost anything
Really?

Depressed

Sad, sad,
But not depressed
What does that mean?
My face does not wear a tragic mask
(Almost never)
But it wears one!
I walk with such speed
You would think I was a track star.
I do all of my errands—and
Wash my hair every day.
I have a positive philosophy
I tell everyone to cheer up . . .
I don't smoke, drink,
Or compulsively eat
Except at 3:00 A.M., when no one is looking.
My skin is free of acne,
My breath is hermetically sealed—I use Binaca daily.
My hair is the latest
Dyed, and cut just right
I smile . . .
Sad, sad, but not depressed.
Now, what does that mean?
It means—it means—I'm dying,
But my mask is on—is yours?

No No's

My Mother
      is not just a Mother
          tho' that would be enough—
My Mother
      is a woman of courage
My Mother
        has strength
        She is the American flag
        independent
        forever hopeful
        like no other. She is proud
          I am her daughter
             and
I am just lucky that I have known her.
      Without her
I would understand no.
      Knowing her
There are No No's
only try again
It could be that she would have been
a lampshade if she understood can't
      Marvelous for me
          she cannot!

Thursday

We stole hours
to be together midweek.
      We stopped at a
      plant shop on the highway.
An odd soup bowl said
to me "take me home"
And you bought it for me
We looked at a
fountain, the kind I
      had as a child
And a funny statue
was spouting water
      into ivy—oh! to
      feel 12 again.
        There was a big
        table—filled
        with sea
        shells
          You tried
to kiss me near the
pots—and I wanted
you to stop—or
didn't I—we have
        never had a day
like today
not in a long time

The kiss in the back of the
        nursery made me
        feel uncomfortable.
        16 years, and
        I was shy?
Marriage and daily
life have really
done a number on
us, haven't they?
Just think how in love
we could be if we ever
pursued it
        But we seem
to want to recapture
something today
        in the woodsy
restaurant where I'd been
a thousand years ago.
We felt warm didn't we?
We were trying for instant romance.
        I noticed there
weren't any married couples
I could just tell
You said all the right things

The ocean so
glorious like
silver blue lame
       And suddenly
       you kissed me
And I liked it
       But then I
       noticed the clock
       Our time was up, the
       vodka had just begun
       to work.
Was it that or
       us?
Or the ocean?
       Never mind
I was sorry as I looked at you
       that we've
wasted so much time fighting and
       not caring
There is still something
special about you—
       Something odd like the
       pot that asked me to
       take it home
         Take me home—now
          Please!

Mother's Day

Mother's Day is supposed to be the day my children honor
  me.
How stupid, how wrong. It is I who should honor them
That I have been allowed by some biological system to give
birth—to give life, the greatest gift of all. There is
no more need for gifts!

Being a Mother allows me to love with complete
selfishness. And a good reason to care for
myself.
>   They have given me joy
>   They have given me pain
>   They give me a chance at immortality . . .
>   what more . . . what more
Motherhood is not always glorious. It is boring and tedious,
and a thief of my heart, and my time.
It gives me a right to worry, grieve, scream, holler, mold,
  swear,
laugh, hate, wonder.
It gives me another childhood.
I hope they'll grow up and really like me.

I have
Two people I really adore—and what a gift that is.
We didn't choose each other but I think
we're making it work.
I hope so
I think I'm going to cry.
Mothers are supposed to.
For Shepsie
And Lisa Beth
Mother's Day '77

Father's Day

Tonight as you sat
     on the round tweed chair
your legs weary with age
It crossed my mind
how young and handsome
       sitting at your big desk, making deals
       you were. So strong. How cruel is time
       How terrible is age.

I see a young man—
       black curly hair, wet with the
       sweat of work, filled with dreams
       of American success

As you got your success
       and the years went by and hair
       whitened, I never saw you
       age. I see it only for a moment
       or two now, and when I do
       I hate it

Time is my enemy
Time is my thief

But time cannot steal the
       Pictures in my head
       indelible forever
       you are still filled with
       incredible dreams and
       for some moments, strong with
       energy, and when
       I see that
          I forget time
          I forget my enemy
          Time is my friend

The clock has stopped
and you are—you again
I wonder today, knowing what
you always do for me
if I have ever done
anything for you, really.

Don't tell me if I haven't.
I couldn't stand it—I
don't have the time!

Women's Lib—Yes or No

Why do we need a movement to prove our worth?
Why do we need lectures, to prove that we know
        what we are?
We are not men
We are women
We do what we do
You do what you do
If we need to work
        You need to pay us our due
If we bear you children
        You need to help us
If you leave us, and we are alone with our children
        We can help ourselves if we must.
There is a place for us
We are not slaves
Neither are you
We are equal
We each have a place
We ask that you are just
        That you give us our due
Some of us know this
Most of you don't
Some of us feel you trap us
If we let you it is our fault

We are not slaves
Neither are you
We have a need for a home
Maybe you do or do not
If we cannot be together
You may go your own way
      You are the child of a mother too
I will not hold you
But you cannot ask me to love you
     if you leave me
      to be alone.
Then I am both of us
I am woman and I am man too!
     And that is not my way.
But I will be
If I have to be
I can be anything
I ask no more than what is due me
     I need you, I do
      I am a woman

Television

Do you know when I was a little girl
I didn't watch television
        because there wasn't any
        We had radio—and music
        and "the movies"
            and families
        We had causes—
            and singing
                And no one I
knew was divorced
        or o.d.'d
        or ran away
        or did anything
            except be
            what they were
                expected to be
There were real heros
        and school
        and plays
        and lessons
            But mostly families
We grew up but then
it wasn't correct to
        expect anything because they had
        the right to do and be what they
        wanted

And they had grown differently
Because when you
were a tiny person
no one watched television
And now
it's taken the place of
company
manners and families
good looks
breeding
knowledge
reading
music
imagination
It's taken care of all of that
with a big screen
and color and
sound
And easy
and at home
and . . . So Boring
No one I knew
went to jail
had a drug problem
or "shrunk" every day

No one did anything they
weren't expected to do
          And then
          we began growing up
               and we saw everything
          we loved it
                    And then somehow
               everyone knew everything
                    And you were lucky
                    if you weren't divorced
                    if your kids didn't o.d.
No! I'm saving television
for my very
          very
          old
          age
When I'm too infirm
to care about anything
else—or maybe
by that time I'll
be dead—and I won't care
Especially
what everyone's missed
               by forever watching television
               Whatever happened to
                    Families?

Yellow Roses

Bar Harbor is cold!
It was summer
I was young, young
They said Sweep the stage, paint the scenery, be an actress
This is stock
This is experience
This is life
I was young, young

The accident—like a movie
They said, Do you know the lines
I don't know . . . I called home . . . And told them
3000 miles away. He hopped a plane to N.Y.
Got dumped in St. Louis. Another plane to Boston
A florist in Boston sold yellow roses
A cab to Bar Harbor, another to Surrey, Maine
He was tired
I was very, very young
I walked onto the stage
I saw him.
all huge and dark and beaming, the roses wilting, my heart
leaping, the play over, the curtain down

He saw me
He saw me
He made it
He came
He cared
I cried!
I was an actress.
Someone gave me roses
Someone cared

This is stock
This is experience
          And he has always, always made it
          No matter what
          My Father.
               Thank You,
               Daddy

               The
               Roses
               Have
               Never
               Wilted

ASTON HALL ROMANCES

From Pinnacle Books

**Wholesome and sophisticated stories
about modern women facing modern dilemmas—
written especially for women like you!**

☐ **41-117-0 A DISTANT SONG #105**
by Iris Bromige
Sarah is torn between the man she loves and the fear she is being used.

☐ **41-118-9 STARFIRE #106**
by Arlene Morgan
Only a secret she can never reveal stands between Peggy and the man she loves.

☐ **41-119-7 DOCTORS IN LOVE #107**
by Sonia Deane
Emma is a doctor whose handsome medical partner wants to mix business with pleasure.

☐ **41-120-0 NO STARS SO BRIGHT #108**
by Mary Faid
Cathy's love for Neil overpowers everything but the barrier between them.

☐ **41-121-9 THE SCENT OF ROSEMARY #109**
by Lorna Hill
For Ellie and the young doctor it's only a holiday affair...until fate intervenes and throws them together again.

☐ **41-122-7 SHETLAND SUMMER #110**
by Audrie Manley-Tucker
Serena is torn between an attractive widower and her handsome employer.

All Books $1.50

Buy them at your local bookstore or use this handy coupon.
Clip and mail this page with your order

⊚ **PINNACLE BOOKS, INC.—Reader Service Dept.**
271 Madison Ave., New York, NY 10016

Please send me the book(s) I have checked above. I am enclosing $_____
(please add 75¢ to cover postage and handling). Send check or money order only—no cash or C.O.D.'s.

Mr./Mrs./Miss _____

Address _____

City_____ State/Zip_____

Please allow six weeks for delivery. Prices subject to change without notice.

The Quotable Woman

1800-the present

compiled and edited by Elaine Partnow

"Both an indispensable reference tool—and a book to dip into and enjoy."
— *Working Woman* magazine

Timeless. Poignant. Entertaining. Now, for the first time in paperback, two unique encyclopedic volumes exclusively devoted to the insights, contemplations and inspirations of over 1300 women—from suffragists to liberationists, authors to educators—that no woman should be without!

☐ 40-859-5 *VOLUME ONE: 1800–1899* $3.95
☐ 40-874-9 *VOLUME TWO: 1900–the present* $3.95

And... *THE QUOTABLE WOMAN* box set—an ideal gift!

☐ 41-050-6 *VOLUMES ONE* and *TWO* $7.90

Buy them at your local bookstore or use this handy coupon.
Clip and mail this page with your order

◎ **PINNACLE BOOKS, INC.—Reader Service Dept.**
271 Madison Ave., New York, NY 10016

Please send me the book(s) I have checked above. I am enclosing $_____ (please add 75¢ to cover postage and handling). Send check or money order only—no cash or C.O.D.'s.

Mr./Mrs./Miss _____

Address _____

City _____ State/Zip _____

Please allow six weeks for delivery. Prices subject to change without notice.